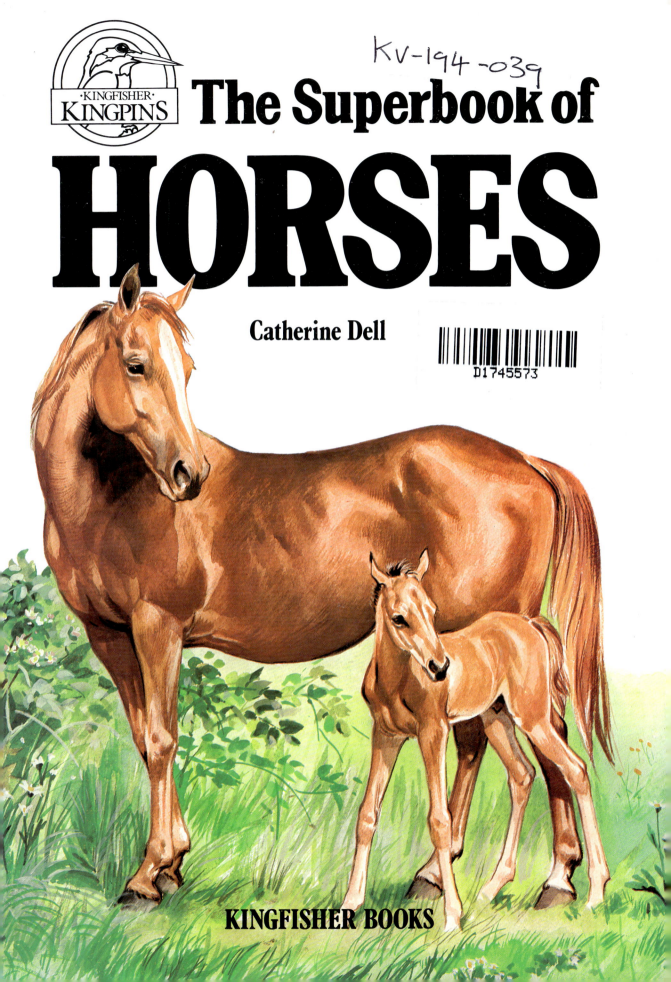

The Superbook of
HORSES

Catherine Dell

KINGFISHER BOOKS

Contents

This revised edition published in 1985 by Kingfisher Books Limited
Elsley Court, 20–22 Great Titchfield Street, London W1P 7AD
A Grisewood & Dempsey Company
Originally published in hardcover by Ward Lock Limited in 1981
in the Wonder Book series.
Reprinted 1987
© Grisewood & Dempsey Limited 1981, 1985

BRITISH LIBRARY CATALOGUING IN PUBLICATION DATA
Dell, Catherine
    Horses. – 2nd ed. – (Kingpins)
    1. Horses – Juvenile literature
    I. Title   II. Dell, Catherine.
    Wonder book of horses
    636.1   SF302

ISBN 0-86272-176-8

Edited by Angela Royston
Designed by Keith Groom
Cover designed by the Pinpoint Design Company
Printed in Hong Kong by the South China Printing Co.

Cover and previous page: Mare with foal.

Horses

A horse is a hoofed, four-footed animal with a flowing mane and tail. But it is also much more than that. That 'hoofed, four-footed animal' has been workmate, ally and companion to people for more than 50 centuries. It has carried them along city streets and country lanes, pulled their carts and wagons, fought with them on the battlefield, ploughed their fields, trekked with them into unknown lands, threshed their corn, and entertained them on the racecourse and in the circus ring. Until the discovery of other sources of power, such as steam and oil, people relied on horses for all kinds of work.

This book traces the story of the horse from the prehistoric swamps of 55 million years ago to the present day and shows how the horse's role has changed from work and war to sport and leisure.

Alexander the Great on his horse, Bucephalus

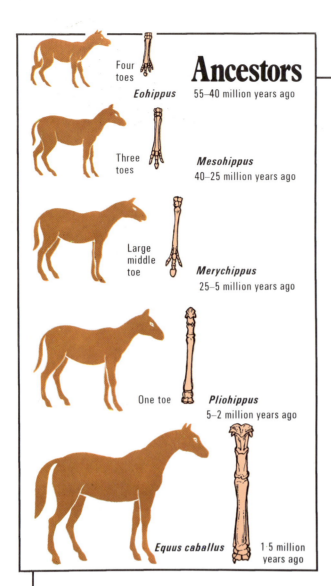

Ancestors

Eohippus
Four toes
55–40 million years ago

Mesohippus
Three toes
40–25 million years ago

Merychippus
Large middle toe
25–5 million years ago

Pliohippus
One toe
5–2 million years ago

Equus caballus
1·5 million years ago

About

The horse has a long history. It began life 55 million years ago as a tiny, striped creature called *Eohippus*, or Dawn Horse. *Eohippus*, living in the swampy, prehistoric jungle, was quite unlike a modern horse. It stood only 25 cm (10 inches) tall, fed on leaves, not grass, and had feet with toes.

As millions of years went by, the land became drier and opened out into grassy plains. *Eohippus'* descendants changed too. They grew larger and stronger and moved out onto the plains. There they learnt to eat grass and to escape enemies by running swiftly on their middle toes. In time, their side toes vanished, leaving just one toe covered by a hard nail or hoof. The first one-toed horse, *Pliohippus*, was the direct ancestor of *Equus caballus*, today's horse.

◄ The horse through time, from fox-sized Eohippus, with short legs and four-toed feet, to modern Equus, with long, powerful legs and one-toed feet protected by hooves. Equus is about eight times taller than Eohippus.

The earliest known pictures of horses were painted by Stone Age people on the walls of caves. These underground paintings were probably not decoration, but hunting magic. Before setting out on a hunt for food, cave people used to draw pictures of their prey to bring them luck in the hunt. Stone Age hunters also believed that the spirits of animals they killed would find a resting place inside the drawings. The horse picture shown here, from a cave in southern France, is about 20,000 years old.

Horses

Equus caballus was over a million years old when modern man came on the scene. From the beginning, people were involved with horses. Primitive peoples hunted them for meat and milk and for skins which they made into clothes and tents. But, about 3000 BC, a wandering tribe in central Asia tamed some wild ponies. At first, these nomads kept the animals for food, but soon they were using them to pull and carry heavy loads. Then the tribesmen discovered how to ride. Now they could hunt, fight and travel on horseback.

The horse habit spread quickly. In ancient China, Persia, Babylon, Egypt and beyond, horses became part of daily life, and legend. One great legendary horse was Pegasus, from Ancient Greece. Pegasus had wings and carried the thunder of Zeus across the sky.

Donkey   Zebra

The Horse Family

The horse has four living relatives. The zebra and the ass are wild; the donkey and the mule are domestic. Zebras, striped black and white, belong to the African plains. Asses come from hot, dry lands in North Africa and Asia. The African ass was the ancestor of the donkey, a small, sure-footed animal that is still used in many countries to carry heavy loads. A male donkey mated with a female horse produces a mule. Mules are very strong and hard-working.

► In cold northern regions, heavy and slow horses fed on rich pastures. Strong work horses, like this Ardennes, come from northern horses.

◄ After the Ice Ages, two types of horse developed. In hot, dry southern lands, where grazing was poor, horses became lightly built, smooth-coated and fast runners. Southern horses were the ancestors of many saddle horses like this Arab.

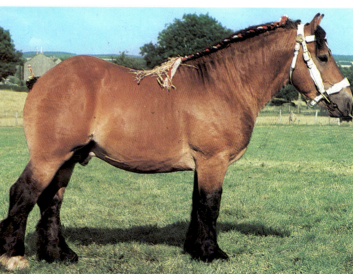

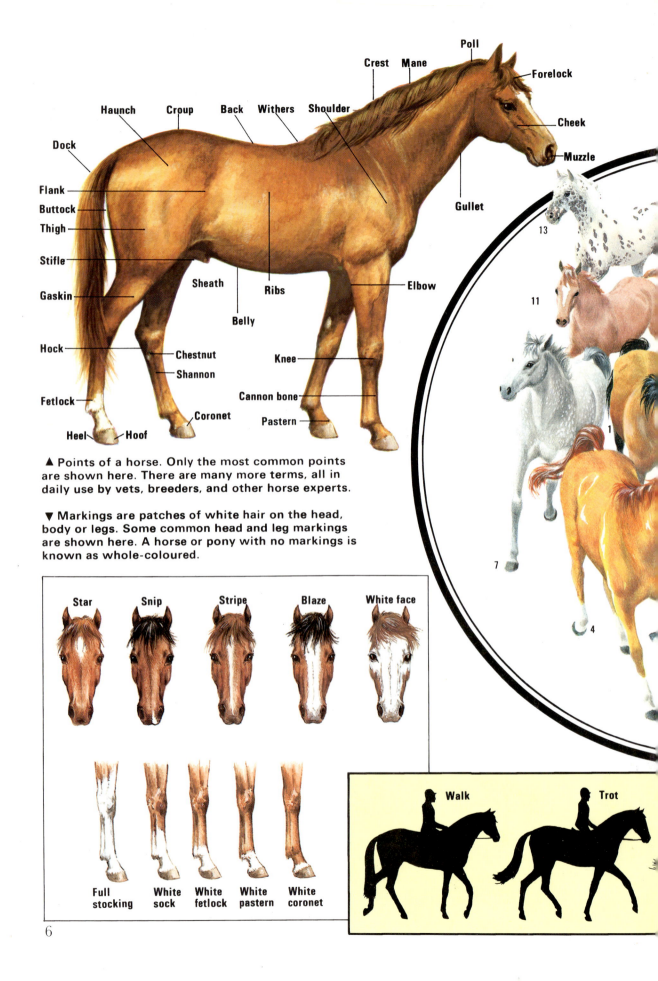

Points of a horse. Poll, Crest, Mane, Forelock, Haunch, Croup, Back, Withers, Shoulder, Cheek, Dock, Muzzle, Flank, Gullet, Buttock, Thigh, Stifle, Sheath, Ribs, Elbow, Gaskin, Belly, Hock, Chestnut, Knee, Shannon, Fetlock, Cannon bone, Coronet, Pastern, Heel, Hoof

▲ Points of a horse. Only the most common points are shown here. There are many more terms, all in daily use by vets, breeders, and other horse experts.

▼ Markings are patches of white hair on the head, body or legs. Some common head and leg markings are shown here. A horse or pony with no markings is known as whole-coloured.

Star, Snip, Stripe, Blaze, White face

Full stocking, White sock, White fetlock, White pastern, White coronet

Walk, Trot

Horse Talk

Measuring Horses

All horses and ponies, except Shetland ponies, are measured in hands from the ground to the top of the withers. A hand is 10 cm (4 inches). Shetlands are measured in inches.

The horse world has its own language. The animals themselves have special names: an adult male horse is called a stallion, an adult female is a mare, and a young horse under a year old is a foal.

The parts of a horse's body such as the mane, muzzle, cheek, chest are known as points. Put together, a horse's points make up its conformation or overall shape. A horse can have good or bad conformation. A hollow back, inward-turning hocks and boxy hoofs are typical of bad conformation.

Horses come in all sizes from the tiny Falabella pony to the giant Shire. Their height is measured in hands; animals under 14.2 hands are ponies. Horses also come in many colours. The five main colours for horses and ponies are black, brown, bay, chestnut and dun; but there are variations.

Finally, horses are divided into types and breeds. A horse's type depends on its size and purpose. It may, for example, be a hunter, carthorse, or polo pony. Breed is like family. Appaloosa, Clydesdale, Criollo are all breeds. A horse with both parents of the same breed is called a pure-bred.

1 **Bay** Brown with black mane and tail
2 **Black** Black
3 **Brown** Dark brown
4 **Chestnut** Red-brown
5 **Cream** Cream colour
6 **Dun** Sandy with black mane and tail
7 **Grey** Mixed black and white hairs
8 **Palomino** Gold with white mane and tail
9 **Piebald** Large black and white patches
10 **Blue roan** Black or brown coat mixed with white hairs; black mane and tail
11 **Strawberry roan** Chestnut coat mixed with white hairs
12 **Skewbald** Patches of white and any colour except black
13 **Spotted** Coloured spots on white or white spots on colour

◄ Horses and ponies have four natural paces: walk, trot, canter, and gallop. At a walk, the horse moves its legs in turn, making four hoof beats. The trot has only two hoof beats as the legs move in pairs. At a canter, there are three beats; two legs move together on the second beat. Galloping, the legs move quickly in succession and make four beats.

Canter

Gallop

Thoroughbreds are the best racehorses in the world. All Thoroughbreds are descended from three Arab stallions: the Byerley Turk, the Darley Arabian and the Godolphin Arabian. These Arabs were brought to Britain around 1700 and crossed with English mares.

Record-breaking Breeds

Shire horses are the largest and heaviest horses in the world. They stand up to 20 hands tall and weigh over a tonne. Shires, and other heavy horses, are the most powerful animals alive after elephants.

Falabella ponies are the smallest members of the horse family. Some are only 4 hands high. Too small to ride, they are bred as pets.

Thoroughbreds are the fastest horses on Earth. On the racecourse they reach speeds of 65 km/h (40 mph). They are also the most valuable: a champion Thoroughbred is worth millions of dollars.

The Specialists

When men and horses became partners, one of the most important things they did together was to wage war. Horses soon became so valuable in battle that opposing armies tried to capture each other's animals. Captured horses were taken back to the enemy's homeland where they were mated with local horses. Gradually, separate breeds began to develop: strong horses for farm work, brave horses for war, fast horses for sport, and so on.

Today there are about 300 different breeds of horses and ponies in the world. The oldest breed is the Arab. Arabs are prized for their beauty, speed, stamina and intelligence. And their antiquity: it is said that the first Arab belonged to Noah's great-great-grandson! During their long history, Arabs have been crossed with many other horses to create new breeds. The greatest breed produced 300 years ago was the Thoroughbred. These proud, elegant stars of the racecourse are the fastest horses alive.

Like Arabs and Thoroughbreds, many breeds were produced for riding and racing. Others were created for work. Heavy horses, such as French Percherons and English Shires, were developed as draught animals to pull ploughs and barges, cannons and carriages. Some ponies, too, are bred for special jobs, such as the Fjord pony which works on mountain farms in Norway. But many ponies become riding animals for children.

◀ The brave, agile Lusitano, from Portugal, was first bred as a cavalry horse. Today, it is widely used for bullfighting. In Portugal, bullfighters are mounted.

▼ Belgian Brabants ploughing. Like other heavy horses, Brabants are descended from the Great Horses of the Middle Ages that were used to carry knights into battle. In time, these mighty beasts became draught animals and separate breeds developed.

Living Wild

The mustangs of North America are brave, hardy animals and very agile. They go back to the conquest of America. In the 1500s, when Spanish adventurers first came to the New World, they brought their horses with them. Before then, there were no horses in America. As the Spaniards explored the land, some of their animals escaped and others were stolen by Indians. These horses lived wild and, with time, grew small and tough: they were the first mustangs. In the days of the Wild West, mustangs were captured and tamed by both Indians and cowboys. Today, they are often used for the bucking bronco event in rodeos.

Wild horses are now so rare they may soon die out completely. The only wild horses alive today are Przewalski's horses, from the bleak Gobi desert of Mongolia.

There are, however, many horses living in a wild state. They are not truly wild because they are descended from domestic breeds—horses that have worked with people. These semi-wild animals include the mustangs of North America, the Camargue horses of France, the Australian brumbies and the ponies of Assateague Island.

The brumbies of the Australian outback began with the gold rush a hundred years ago. Many Australian farmers left their farms, set their horses loose and went in search of gold.

The Atlantic island of Assateague is famous for its wild skewbald ponies. Their ancestors were shipwrecked, centuries ago, on their way from North Africa to Peru.

Przewalski's Horse

Przewalski's horses, the only true wild horses, are small sturdy creatures with a rough sandy coat and a dark stripe along the back. Their name comes from the Russian explorer, Colonel Przewalski, who found them in 1881. In Mongolia, the horses are still hunted and very few remain. Soon, they will only exist in museums and zoos.

▶ Carmargue horses at home in the shallow marsh waters of the Rhône delta. Their ancestors probably came here from the Middle East with the Saracen invaders in the 700s. These small tough horses now spend most of their life running wild; but many are used by French cowboys, called *gardiens*, for herding cattle.

Horses in History

The Roman Emperor Caligula and his horse, Incitatus.

When the horse died, Alexander built a city called Bucephala in its memory. (See also page 22.)

One of the most pampered horses in history was Incitatus, the favourite horse of the Roman Emperor Caligula. Incitatus was kept in an ivory stall in a marble stable and wore a jewelled collar and purple blankets, the colour of royalty. It was said by some people that Caligula had even made his horse consul, a very high rank in Roman government!

Napoleon Bonaparte on his horse, Marengo.

Horses have played an important part in history. Many explorers, soldiers and other great heroes have had horses that helped them to carry out their deeds

One of the most famous horses in history was made of wood. About 3500 years ago, the Ancient Greeks attacked the city of Troy in Asia Minor. They built a huge wooden horse and left it outside the gates of Troy. The Trojans thought the horse was sacred and would protect them. They dragged the horse through the gates and into the city. But late that night, when all the Trojans were asleep, a small band of Greek soldiers crept out of the horse. They opened the city gates for the rest of the Greek army, which rushed in and captured the city.

Alexander the Great was a ruler of Greece and one of the greatest generals in history. He conquered a huge empire that stretched from the Mediterranean Sea to India. Even when Alexander was young he was brave and fearless. He tamed the beautiful horse Bucephalus, which no one else dared to ride. Bucephalus carried Alexander on his many long journeys.

The French Emperor Napoleon's horse Marengo was a grey Arab stallion. The horse was named after a famous battle that Napoleon's army fought and won. After Napoleon's defeat at Waterloo, Marengo was brought to Britain and today his skeleton can be seen at the National Army Museum in London. (See also page 22.)

General Robert E. Lee led the Confederate Army during the American Civil War. His horse, Traveller, was a big grey, part Thoroughbred, part Morgan. Traveller fought many battles with Lee and was never wounded. The horse was Lee's constant companion until the general's death.

Alexander the Great on Bucephalus.

General Robert E. Lee on his horse, Traveller.

Racing

Horses for

The people of Ancient Egypt, Greece and Rome loved going to the races. And races then meant chariot races: swirling dust, cracking whips, thundering hoofs and speeding wheels. Chariot racing was the very first horse sport. Today, it still happens, but with stricter rules and a new name:

harness racing. In harness racing, horses go at a quick trot (not a canter or gallop), pulling light, two-wheeled carriages called gigs or sulkies.

Horse-racing, with a mounted jockey, is almost as old as harness racing and is mentioned in the records of the 648 BC Olympics. Since then, it has grown into a popular sport and a big business. There are just two kinds of horse-racing: flat racing and steeplechasing. Flat races are run on the flat, on either turf or dirt tracks. They take place in summer when the ground is hard and fast. In a steeplechase, the course includes fences and other obstacles. Steeplechasing is a winter sport as the ground is then softer and so safer for jumping.

▲ A Roman chariot race. The chariots raced in teams, known by their colours: the Blues, Reds, Greens and Whites. Spectators, including the emperor, had favourite teams and, like modern race-goers, placed bets.

► Harness racing is popular in the USA and Russia and both countries have developed a special breed for the event: the American Standardbred and the Orlov Trotter, shown here. During the Russian winter, sledges are often used instead of gigs.

Sport

▲ Steeplechasing began in the 1700s when country squires raced each other across the fields, jumping over hedges and ditches on the way. They raced from the church steeple of one village to the next; hence the name of steeplechasing.

Jockeys wear brightly coloured shirts and caps called silks. Each jockey wears the colours of the horse's owner. Jockeys are small and light so that they do not slow down the horse. In the 1800s, a jockey called Kitchener weighed only 20 kg (44 lb).

▼ Flat racing. Some great flat races are the Derby and St Leger in England, the Melbourne Cup in Australia and the US Kentucky Derby.

◄ Clearing a parallel bar in a show-jumping competition. During a jump, the rider bends forward following the horse's movement. Through television, show jumping has become a popular spectator sport and millions of people enjoy the skill and excitement of a contest. Highlights of the show-jumping year include the Horse of the Year Show in London, the National Horse Show in New York and Germany's Aachen Show.

Upright rails

Jumping and Eventing

As a sport, show jumping is quite modern. It involves jumping a series of man-made obstacles, arranged in a set order. If a horse knocks a fence down, or refuses to jump, its rider is penalized with a number of faults. At the end of the competition, if the leading riders all have clear rounds (no faults), or the same number of faults, they complete the course again to decide the winner. This is called a jump-off. Sometimes the jump-off is against the clock in which case the fastest round with the least faults wins.

Show jumping also forms part of another competition called eventing. Eventing originated with the training of cavalry horses. These horses had to be strong, agile, and fit, able to gallop for many kilometres, able to jump any obstacle and, most important, they had to be totally obedient. Eventing tests all these qualities. The competition has three parts: dressage, cross-country, and show jumping. All three parts can take place on the same day or be spread over two or three days. A three-day event is very tough.

Show Jumping

▼ A selection of show-jumping fences. The rails, wall and gate are all upright fences. The hog's back, water jump and oxer are spread fences. In the hog's back, the middle pole is higher than the other two; an oxer is a hedge with poles at take-off and landing. A show-jumping course is full of sharp bends to test the horse's ability to jump a straight fence right after a turn. Fences are usually close together.

Fancy gate

Wall

Water jump

Hog's back

Oxer

Dressage

Dressage, a French word for schooling or training, tests a horse's obedience and skill. In a dressage competition, the horse must carry out different paces and movements, including circles and turns. A good dressage horse obeys its rider's instructions quickly, and performs each movement with control and precision. Throughout the competition, rider and horse must move together smoothly. They must also be well turned-out, as smart appearance is part of the test.

Cross-country is the most exciting and most difficult part of eventing. The competition takes place over a long course that contains many natural obstacles like water splashes, high hedges, wide ditches, steep banks, stone walls, and piled-up logs. Completing this type of course at speed is an immense test of courage and strength for both horse and rider.

Despite their name, polo ponies, at 15 hands high, are really horses. Most are bred from Argentinian cow ponies and are trained to move, turn and stop quickly. Polo ponies wear bandages to protect their legs from swinging mallets.

A Sporting Life

The world of horse sport spreads far beyond the racecourse and the show-jumping arena. It includes many different games and activities, some of them thousands of years old.

In the beginning, horse sports often had a purpose. Fox-hunting, for example, grew out of the farmer's need to destroy animal pests. Many others were developed by armies to train mounted soldiers. In battle, cavalry had to stop suddenly, turn and move off quickly. Games such as tent-pegging and polo gave horse and rider practice in these skills. Tent-pegging contests were popular in the 1800s. Each rider, going at a gallop, had to pull a tent peg from the ground with his lance. This was not at all easy!

Polo, called the fastest team game in the world, probably came from Ancient Persia. Today, it is played in most countries—and not just by soldiers. In a polo match, two teams of four riders try to score by driving a wooden ball into their opponents' goal. They use a wooden mallet with a long handle to hit the ball. The game is divided into six seven-minute periods called chukkas. As polo is played at a non-stop gallop, most horses are tired out after two chukkas. So each rider needs at least three animals.

Another famous, but controversial, sport involving horses is bullfighting. Horses ridden by bullfighters have to be brave and agile to escape the angry attacks of the bull.

In Ancient China, hunting on horseback was a popular sport for rich people. They hunted all kinds of animals, using dogs, cheetahs or falcons in the chase, then bows and arrows.

A drag-hunt. In drag-hunting, hounds and huntsmen follow a man-made trail instead of an animal. The trail is laid with a strong-smelling substance such as aniseed. Drag-hunting has replaced fox-hunting in many places.

Going Places

In the Middle Ages, riding was part of everyday life. The rich, like this nobleman, rode fine, handsome horses; ordinary people had small, scruffy animals.

Before the days of cars, buses, and trains, land transport meant horses. People usually travelled on horseback or in horse-drawn vehicles—or they walked. During five thousand years of history, horses have pulled all kinds of vehicles: war chariots in the ancient world; heavy carts trundling goods in the Middle Ages; dazzling carriages of kings and queens; covered wagons taking pioneers across America; stage-coaches carrying passengers and mail from town to

A painting of horse-drawn traffic dashing through Central Park, New York, in the 1860s. By this time, closed carriages had glass windows to keep out the wind and rain.

Horses

town; canal barges loaded with grain, stone, coal; and double-decker omnibuses. Horses even helped the transport revolution that finally overtook them: the first steam trains needed horses to pull them uphill.

In the beginning, riding itself was unpopular because it was uncomfortable: early horsemen rode bareback. But soon, saddles appeared; then much later, around 400 AD, came stirrups. These made the going much easier for both rider and horse.

Horses were often a mark of rank. This Chinese official, travelling with such elegance, must have been important.

Two of the horse's relatives, mules and donkeys, still work hard in many countries. These donkeys in Morocco take their owners, with baskets of produce, to and from market.

War-horses

Heroes in Battle

Some of history's most famous horses have been war-horses.

● Bucephalus, the mighty horse hero of ancient times, belonged to Alexander the Great. Alexander, on Bucephalus, led a huge conquering army across half the world. When the horse died, in 326 BC, Alexander built a city over its grave and called it Bucephala.

● Two thousand years later, another great emperor, Napoleon, also had a famous horse. Marengo, a small, grey Arab, carried Napoleon from victory to victory—until Waterloo. After the Emperor's defeat, Marengo was captured and taken to England. At Waterloo, Wellington's horse, Copenhagen, was just as amazing: over 17 hours in the battlefield and yet the chestnut Thoroughbred showed no sign of tiredness.

● But the most famous war-horse of all was a giant wooden horse made by the Ancient Greeks. Greek soldiers hid inside the horse as part of a plan to capture the enemy city of Troy.

Ancient armies soon discovered that if they fought on horseback, instead of on foot, they were more likely to win. So, from the time of the Assyrians right up to World War II, horses were man's allies on the battlefield.

Early warriors, carrying a spear or bow and arrow, rode swift, agile animals. But in the Middle Ages, fighting changed. Knights and horses wore huge suits of armour. In time, armour became too heavy, making the horses slow and clumsy. So techniques changed again. By the 1700s, fast mounted soldiers, or cavalry, armed with only a sword or lance, formed the main fighting force.

Modern weapons put an end to battles on horseback. At the last big cavalry charge, near Moscow during World War II, 2000 Russian horsemen were gunned down.

The Ancient Assyrians, with their war chariots, were the first people to use horses in battle.

▲ In the Middle Ages, armoured knights and their horses took part in war games called tournaments and jousts, where they fought mock battles to test their skill and courage.

▼ French and English cavalrymen fighting at Waterloo. When the two cavalries charged, the French went at a trot, the British galloped.

► When American Indians went into battle wearing war paint and feathers, their horses were often painted too. Each mark had a special meaning.

◄ This drum horse, Cicero, is a well-known member of the Life Guards; he has even had a film made about him and his work. Now that wars are no longer fought by soldiers on horseback, military horses like Cicero are mainly kept for ceremonial purposes.

Below left: Police horses help maintain law and order in most of the world's big cities. Here, a mounted London policewoman uses her horse to hold back a crowd of tourists outside Buckingham Palace. From her high position, she can also watch the crowd's growth and movement.

▼ In some parts of the world, horse-drawn taxis are for everybody, not just tourists. This gharry takes passengers through the bustling streets of New Delhi in India. With horse-drawn vehicles, there are no flat batteries or ignition problems on a cold morning.

In the City

A hundred years ago, a big city had almost as many horses as people. They were everywhere, pulling coaches, carriages, omnibuses, trams, cabs, dust carts, furniture vans, fire engines, ambulances, funeral hearses, and the many delivery carts belonging to tradesmen such as butchers, bakers, milkmen, grocers, fishmongers, and coal merchants. The streets were noisy with rattling wheels, cracking whips, clattering hooves, and drivers' shouts.

Today, streets are filled with the roar of motor traffic and the haze of exhaust fumes. Even so, there are still horses earning their keep in many big towns and cities. Often, horse-drawn carriages are used as a tourist attraction to take visitors on sightseeing trips. Tourists also love to watch military horses at work. Cameras click as these superb animals march round the parade ground, stand guard outside a palace, or take part in state ceremonies.

Police horses are in the same class. From Buenos Aires to Barcelona, Tehran to Tokyo, police horses are used to control crowds: rival fans on a football pitch, cheering well-wishers along a royal route, or an angry demonstration.

In places, horses still pull delivery carts. One traditional horse-drawn load is beer, carried in barrels on low, open wagons called drays. As petrol prices rise, perhaps other industries will copy the breweries and go back to horses.

▶ Heavy horses pulling a beer dray. This special parade of cart horses is held every year in Regent's Park, London.

In the Country

The sturdy Finnish Horse still takes an active part in country life in its native Finland. It does all kinds of jobs: drawing ploughs, hauling timber, driving village people to market and pulling heavy loads like this sledge piled with building stones. Finnish Horses, usually chestnut, are hard-working animals with kind, sensible natures.

Shire horses at work on a farm. Shire horses, from England, are the strongest horses in the world. Before mechanization, Shires were very common work horses in both town and country. Like many breeds of heavy horse, Shires carry a lot of feather — long hair round the cannon bone and fetlock.

Horses belong to the country and there, in the fields and forests, plains and prairies, many are still working.

For centuries, farmers relied on horse power. Horses pulled ploughs and wagons and turned simple machines like corn mills and butter churns. These farm horses were huge, strong beasts. They came from the medieval Great Horses that were bred to carry armoured knights into battle. With the invention of modern machinery, most farm horses lost their jobs. But not all.

Horses are often used by farmers in mountain country where the slopes are too steep for tractors; and by farmers with only a little land who cannot afford costly equipment such as harvesters. These powerful horses also work with lumbermen, dragging timber through the forests.

Across the world, away from forests and mountains, there are great open grasslands. In places like Argentina, America and Australia, these vast grassy plains are used for stock farming. Here, on a stock farm, or ranch, horses play an important part.

They are used to round up the cattle and sheep and to herd them from one grazing ground to another. Horses ridden by cowboys and stockmen must be quick, agile, and strong. They are trained to 'cut' or single out an animal from the herd and to help the rider when he ropes it. They stop dead immediately a steer has been lassoed and then throw their weight against the struggling animal. Stock horses, and their riders, must have immense stamina. Cattle ranges often stretch for hundreds of kilometres and a cowboy may have to ride for days at a time.

Cowboy Horses

In the world's great cattle countries, cowhands have special names and ride special horses. The North American cowboy often rides a Quarter horse (named after a traditional quarter-mile race that it always won). South of the border, Mexican *vaqueros* like to work on fiery, independent mustangs. South again, in Argentina, *gauchos* prefer the Criollo, a tough little cow pony. Half-way round the globe, Australian stockmen generally use Walers, hardy animals bred by early settlers.

In Australia, cowboys are called stockmen and ranches are cattle stations. Here a stockman is collecting up a runaway calf.

The Entertainers

The bareback-bronco event at a rodeo. The bareback rider, hanging onto a strap, has to stay on the bucking horse for eight seconds. He must also spur the horse to buck more fiercely.

Horses are natural entertainers. They love having an audience—and hearing its applause! This is especially true under the big top where horses have been star performers for hundreds of years. Some circus horses appear in the ring without riders. These are Liberty horses: they carry out a sequence of graceful movements directed by their trainer on the ground. Other circus horses are taught to canter round and round while acrobats perform balancing acts on their backs.

Rodeos are another great horse spectacular. They began about a hundred years ago in the cattle lands of North America. Each year, after rounding up their herds at the railhead, the cowboys got together to have some fun. They often held friendly contests to show off their riding and herding skills. These displays were the first rodeos.

Today, rodeos are big business with huge prizes and many daring events. Some, like calf-roping, come from the cowboy's work on the ranch. Others, like bull-riding and steer-wrestling, were specially planned for rodeos. In steer-wrestling, the cowboy grabs a bull by the horns and wrestles it to the ground; in bull-riding, he rides bareback on a bucking bull for at least eight seconds.

Circuses began as chariot races in Ancient Rome. Since then, horses have always been part of the circus scene. This horse belongs to the Munich Crown Circus.

Lipizzaners

In the 1500s several great riding academies were founded to train cavalry horses and riders. The oldest and most famous academy is the Spanish Riding School in Vienna. The school uses beautiful, pure white horses called Lipizzaners. Their name comes from the town of Lipizza, now in Italy, where they were first bred 400 years ago. At the Spanish Riding School, Lipizzaners are taught *haute école*—advanced paces and movements like intricate turns and spectacular leaps.

Learning to Ride

Controlling a Horse

A rider controls his horse and tells it what to do by using special signals or aids. There are two kinds of aids: natural and artificial. The natural aids are the voice, legs, hands, and body. Artificial aids include spurs and whips. Beginners do not normally use artificial aids; it is more helpful for them to concentrate on natural aids, learning how to apply them correctly.

● **Voice** Horses and ponies like being talked to and can tell the difference between praise and reprimand. The rider should never shout.

● **Legs** The energy that drives a horse forward, called impulsion, comes from its hindquarters. A rider holds his legs firmly against the horse's side and with a light squeeze builds up impulsion.

● **Hands** The rider's hands communicate with the horse through the reins and bit. They yield to increase speed, and close in, without pulling, to decrease speed or change pace downwards.

● **Body** In an upright position, the rider's body weight helps drive the horse forward.

In the fourth century BC, a Greek cavalry officer called Xenophon wrote a book on horsemanship. For centuries, Xenophon's book was a riding best-seller and even today many of his theories and principles are still accepted. Xenophon's success shows that right from the start, people realized riding was a skill that had to be learnt.

The best way of learning to ride is to take lessons from a qualified instructor at a

This rider is relying on the natural aids—voice, legs, hands, and body—to direct her horse. Hand aids control forward movement after it has been built up by the rider's legs; so legs should act before hands.

In the distance, a horse walks over trotting poles. Poles are the first stage in learning to jump: they teach a horse to lift its feet and control its stride.

Your Own

riding school. The first lessons are very important: how to mount, dismount, sit, balance, and hold the reins. Only when beginners have mastered these basic techniques can they safely go on to the paces and halt. Young riders seldom use the gallop; they concentrate on the walk, trot and canter and learn how to move smoothly from one pace to another and back again to the halt. Early sessions often include exercises to make the muscles used in riding relaxed and supple; otherwise, they may become stiff.

Many lessons later, when a rider feels confident on the flat and has complete control of his horse, he is ready to begin jumping. In a jump, the horse goes through four phases: approach, take-off, suspension (in the air), and landing. At every stage, the rider must follow the horse's movement and yet be in total command of the situation. Balance is all important.

Pony Trekking

Pony trekking is a splendid way of having a holiday on horseback. Many trekking holidays are based on centres where groups ride out each day and return at night. But some holidays, for more experienced riders, feature one long ride lasting several days with overnight stops along the route. Native ponies, like Haflingers in Austria and Fjord ponies in Norway, often make good trekking mounts.

After trotting poles, the beginner starts to jump over practice fences called cavaletti. Cavaletti are long poles fixed to X-shaped wooden supports; their height is changed by turning the supports over. Later, cavaletti can be stacked to make much higher or broader fences.

Mounting and Dismounting

Mounting

Horses and ponies do not always respond quickly to learning something new. But once they have been taught with patience and kindness they seldom forget. The early lessons teaching a horse to stand still at the halt are repaid over and over again when the time comes to mount or dismount.

Before mounting, check that the girth is tight so as to avoid the saddle slipping round when you take hold.

Stand with your left shoulder against the horse's head, holding the reins in your left hand. Take the near-side leather in your right hand and place your left foot into the stirrup.

Hold firmly to the reins, placing your right hand on the cantle of the saddle. Now swing your body up and, making sure the toes of your left foot are pointing downwards, throw your right leg over the horse's quarters. Lower yourself gently into the saddle and put your right foot into the stirrup. Sit well down, and take

MOUNTING
1. Stand with your shoulder against the horse's head.
2. Hold the leather with your right hand and place your left foot into the stirrup.
3. With your right hand take hold of the cantle and raise yourself from the ground.
4. Swing up and over, taking care not to kick the horse as you do so!

the reins in both hands. At this stage the leathers may require some adjustment, or the girth may need tightening.

Dismounting

To dismount a horse or pony you do not reverse the mounting procedure. Once you have come to a halt, remove your feet from the stirrups. Hold the reins quite firmly in your left hand and bring your right hand back to the cantle of the saddle. Then, taking the body weight on to your arms – the left hand, with the reins, will be resting at the front of the saddle – swing your right leg over the quarters and vault to the ground, landing on your toes.

You will now be facing the near-side of the horse, still holding the reins in your left hand.

Having dismounted, run up the stirrup irons on both sides, return to the near-side and loosen the girth. Take the reins quietly over the horse's head and lead him back to his stable before unsaddling.

1

DISMOUNTING
1. First remove your feet from the stirrups. This ensures that if the horse moves while you are dismounting, it cannot drag you.
2. Hold the reins in your left hand and swing your right leg over the hindquarters.
3. Vault to the ground, landing on the toes.

2   3

The Paces

THE WALK: After mounting, check the girth and sit well down in the centre of the saddle. Keep your back straight but relaxed, and look ahead. The knees and thighs should be close to the saddle, with the lower parts of the legs free. Rest the balls of the feet against the bars of the stirrups, with the heels lower than the toes. Apply and keep a light contact with the pony's mouth. To move forward, squeeze the lower parts of the legs against the pony's sides, slightly behind the girth. Maintain contact with your hands and adjust your body weight. Next, slightly 'open' your hands, bringing the pony up to the bit, and move off. To bring your pony back to the halt, sit well into the saddle and straighten your spine. Close the lower part of your legs and keep an even pressure. 'Close' the hands to bring the pony back to the bit. The pressure of your legs and the resistance felt through the bit bring the pony to a halt position. He should then stand quietly and square.

THE TROT: To move from a walk to a trot, increase pressure with the lower part of the legs. Shorten the reins to bring your pony well up to the bit. As he responds, squeeze your legs to hold the pace. Next ease the reins but keep contact with the pony's mouth. The two ways of riding at a trot are the 'sitting' and 'rising' positions. The sitting trot is used when making the transition from the trot to another pace. In the rising trot, keep a straight back and do not lean forward. Grip well with the thighs and knees. Your legs must remain quite still against the pony's sides.

THE CANTER: To move from the trot to the canter, increase pressure with both legs behind the girth. Sit well down in the saddle and keep the pony well up to the bit. When cantering, keep close contact with the saddle. The pony should move into his stride with the foreleg leading. A pony is cantering 'disunited' or 'false' when, in moving to the left, the off-fore leads or, to the right, the near-fore leads. The incorrect use of the rider's body weight easily upsets the pace of a canter. Do not lean too far forward or you may lose full control and the pony will tend to move on too quickly and unevenly. The canter is the most difficult pace to perform well and both pony and rider need plenty of practice.

THE GALLOP: The gallop is a pace seldom used by the younger rider. In this pace the rider adopts a forward position, with his weight as near as possible to the centre of gravity. The rider's body weight should be taken on the knees and stirrups. At all times the rider must be in control. Never let the horse take over. There is nothing worse than seeing a rider galloping on when it is obvious that he is being *taken* at this pace. When the going is good or when riding over sands, a gallop can be enjoyed by both pony and rider. At all four paces it is essential that the rider, by using the correct aids, keeps control and is able to move through the paces and back to the halt without undue stress on the pony.

WALK

TROT

CANTER

GALLOP

Looking After a Horse

Horses can be kept out at grass or in a stable. Either way they need a lot of attention. To begin with, they must have food and water. For half the year, a grass-kept horse usually gets enough to eat from grazing, but in autumn and winter it requires extra food such as hay, oats, and bran. Stabled horses need regular feeds throughout the day.

Another vital part of horse care is grooming. This keeps the horse clean, helps it stay fit and healthy, and improves its appearance.

A stable-kept horse must be groomed thoroughly every day. A horse at grass needs less grooming, especially in winter when heavy brushing would remove the natural grease that keeps it warm and dry.

All horses need new shoes, perhaps as often as every six weeks. The horny outside, or wall, of the hoof grows quickly and can outgrow the shoe. If this growth is not cut away, the horse goes lame. So the wall is trimmed and the horse reshod.

When a horse is kept out at grass, regular checks must be made to see that fences and hedges are secure, that no poisonous plants are growing in the field, and that the water trough is full. A grass-kept horse also likes a friendly visit—otherwise it feels lonely!

The farrier, or blacksmith, nails on a new shoe. A horse must have healthy feet: they should be inspected every day, cleaned with a hoof pick, and then oiled with hoof oil.

Grooming

A grooming kit contains a variety of equipment. Dandy brushes are for removing dried mud and dirt; body brushes for brushing the coat, mane, and tail (the brush is cleaned with a curry comb after every stroke); and water brushes are for laying the mane and tail and for washing the hooves. The hoof pick is used to take out stones and mud from the feet. The stable rubber shines the coat.

Tack, like saddles and bridles, also has to be cleaned. It is first washed and dried. Leather parts are then rubbed with saddle soap and metal parts are treated with metal polish.

Water brush

Dandy brush

Body brush

Hoof pick

Curry comb

Metal polish

Comb

Sponge

Duster

Saddle soap

Stable rubber

Looking after a stabled horse involves a lot of work. Every day, the animal must be fed, watered, groomed, and exercised. The stable itself also has to be cleaned or mucked out. Mucking out takes place each morning: the horse's bedding straw is shaken up, dirty straw is removed, and fresh straw put down. This girl is sweeping out soiled straw while the boy carries in a clean supply. Hay hangs in a net in the corner and a bucket of water stands near the door.

Tack

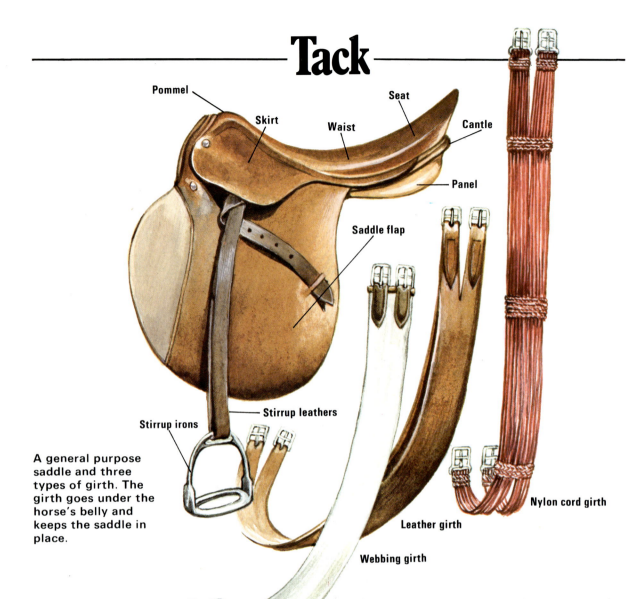

Pommel

Skirt

Seat

Waist

Cantle

Panel

Saddle flap

Stirrup leathers

Stirrup irons

A general purpose saddle and three types of girth. The girth goes under the horse's belly and keeps the saddle in place.

Leather girth

Nylon cord girth

Webbing girth

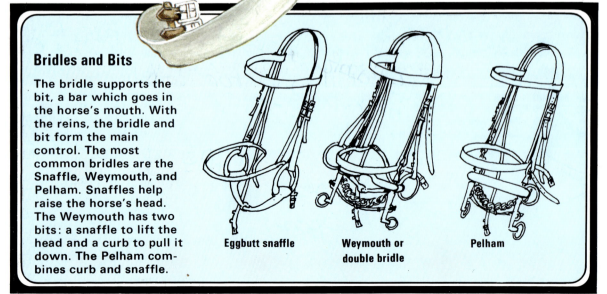

Bridles and Bits

The bridle supports the bit, a bar which goes in the horse's mouth. With the reins, the bridle and bit form the main control. The most common bridles are the Snaffle, Weymouth, and Pelham. Snaffles help raise the horse's head. The Weymouth has two bits: a snaffle to lift the head and a curb to pull it down. The Pelham combines curb and snaffle.

Eggbutt snaffle

Weymouth or double bridle

Pelham

Index

Numbers in **bold type** refer to illustrations.

Acknowledgements

Photographs: 4 Jean Vertut; 5 Sally Anne Thompson *bottom left* and *right;* 9 Spectrum *left,* Fred Spencer *right;* 11 Bruce Coleman *top,* Zefa *bottom;* 14 Sally Anne Thompson; 15 E. D. Lacey; 16 Sally Anne Thompson; 17 Kit Houghton; 19 Zefa; 20 Mansell Collection; 21 J. Allan Cash; 24 British Tourist Authority *top,* Metropolitan Police *bottom;* 25 British Tourist Authority *left,* Zefa *right;* 26 Sally Anne Thompson; 29 Zefa *top* and *bottom;* 31 British Tourist Authority; 36 Kit Houghton; 37 Sally Anne Thompson.

Picture research: Penny Warn.